Sound Doctrine
Outreach Ministries Inc.

Written & Un-Edited by Darick Spears

Sound Doctrine Outreach Ministries Inc.

ISBN: 9781798936269

Printed in USA by DDS MediaWorks LLC./21st Century Shakespears Publishing

Sound Doctrine
Outreach Ministries Inc.

2 Timothy 4:3-4

For the time will come when they will not endure sound doctrine; but after their own lusts shall they heap to themselves teachers, having itching ears; And they shall turn away their ears from the truth, and shall be turned unto fables.

Sound Doctrine is more than a name. It is a term used that the describes **"the hearing of the truth."** Spreading the Gospel of Jesus Christ is not an easy thing to do.

Humans have a way of trying to establish a bargaining relationship with one another, in order to make their agendas fit. But with God's word, there is no time for agendas. The Bible speaks for itself, and as men and women we have a choice to believe or not to believe.

Once we have accepted Christ, then we have a handbook in our possession which is called the Bible. This is the true roadmap to heaven. Some may ask, "Why go to church then if I already have the Bible?"

And my answer is simple, "just because a student has a textbook in their hands, does it make them able to read?" God has placed teachers, shepherds, ministers, missionaries within the doors of the church to help many to understand the Bible. It is not an easy road to walk as a Christian; and it's definitely not easy to walk alone. Brotherhood and sisterhood are important, as well as having a leader who guides the church in truth.

Hebrews 10:25

Not forsaking our own assembling together, as is the habit of some, but encouraging one another; and all the more as you see the day drawing near.

The Mission

Sound Doctrine Outreach Ministries mission is to provide the world with the principle teachings of the Holy Bible. To follow the instructions of Jesus Christ who laid the foundation through his disciples, who gave up their own lives to get out his message.

We will continue to teach, reach, and preach, the Gospel of Jesus Christ, without adding or subtracting from the Bible that was left to be our roadmap to heaven.

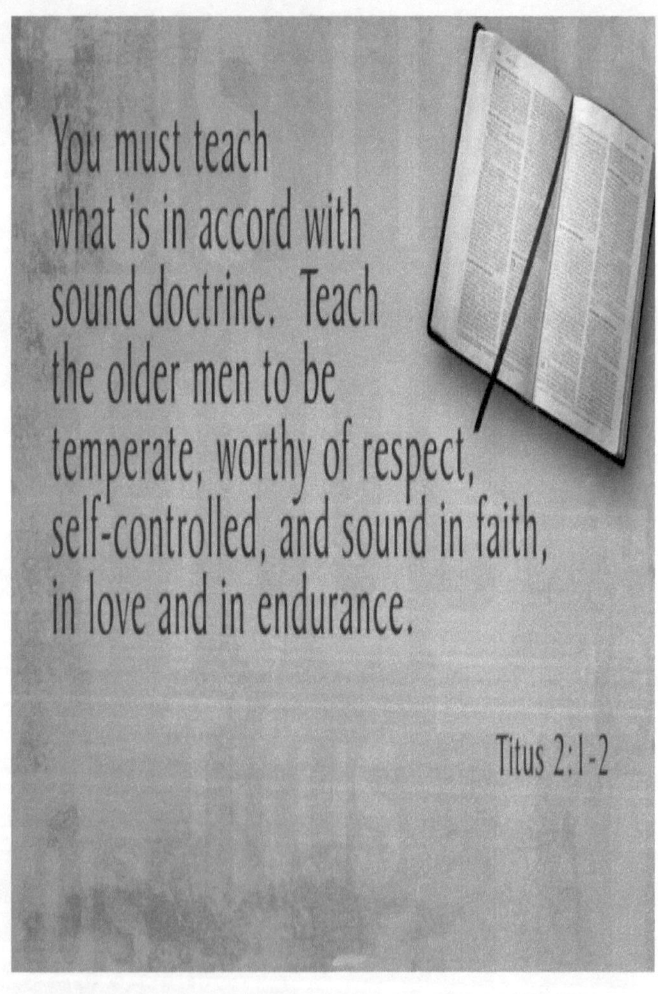

Our Ministry

Spreading the true Gospel, which is the good news according to Jesus Christ; and to provide nothing but Sound Doctrine which is a valuable heritage that is to be treasured in this generation and faithfully transmitted to the next.

Our ministry is built on the foundation of preaching and living by true *sound doctrine*.

According to Paul, doctrine is among the things that matters most for the well-being of the Christian and the

church. Sound, or "healthy," doctrine

provides a pattern that, when

followed, promotes healthy faith and

love.

1 Corinthians 12:28

And God has appointed in the church, first apostles, second prophets, third teachers, then miracles, then gifts of healings, helps, administrations, various kinds of tongues.

Purpose

The purpose of the church is to
be the building stone of faith, love,
and hope through the vision of Jesus
Christ.

We reach out into our communities
and provide teaching, training, love,
peace, and an open invitation for
people to receive salvation through
Jesus Christ.

A church building is a meeting-
ground, where lost souls can be
taught, cleansed, and empowered to

enter the world and be the salt of the earth.

We ask ourselves daily, "What is my purpose?" The simple answer can be found through seeking the higher calling which is in Jesus Christ; for he will guide you to what your true purpose in this life is.

Leadership/Founders

Sound Doctrine Ministries was formed/founded by Pastor Dennis Ray Spears Sr & First Lady Lori Ann Spears. Called by God at age 19, Pastor Dennis Ray Spears Sr., was not raised in a church. He was raised on the farms of Ripley, Mississippi, where he survived a tough childhood.

Not knowing his father, and being raised by his mother, Dennis quickly became the man of the house. In the house with his older brother and younger sister, Pastor Spears Sr.,

knew what he wanted to do in life

early. He wanted to get married and

have a family that he would take care

of.

At age 10, he already had a full-

time job, and was very responsible and

determined. He and his immediate

family would soon migrate from

Mississippi, and find themselves in

Milwaukee, WI. It didn't take him long

to find the love of his life Lori

Murphy, an education, and a bright

starting future. Always determined, he

did the best he could with his hands,
and the limited knowledge he had
obtained.

By age 19, he was already with
the love of his life and expecting a
child. One day, while sitting in an
attic with some friends, smoking weed,
he was moved to leave the room. As he
walked down a flight of stairs, he
heard a voice speaking to him saying
"You are on your way to hell."

He began to see flames, and this
scared him. Miraculously, the next

day he ran into an older lady who
asked him, "Do you want to go to
church?" He took this invitation, and
accepted Christ into his life.

Lori Murphy, who was then his
girlfriend and expecting baby mother;
was already involved in the church.
Wanting to live right, they both
decided to marry, and they haven't
turned back since.

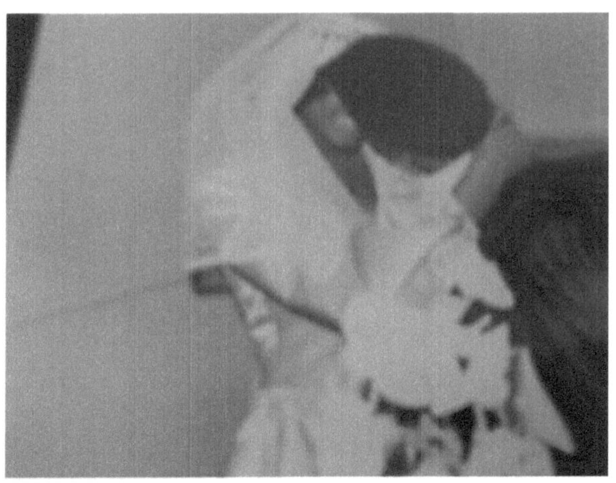

Recently, celebrating 41 years of marriage, as well as 41 years of being saved, sanctified, and filled with the Holy Ghost.

This is just a piece of their story, and they live to serve Jesus, as well the communities of people who need to know Jesus.

The Outreach

Serving the community is a very important mission of *Sound Doctrine Outreach Ministries*. First-Lady, Lori Spears, has owned a daycare center for over 25 years, and has also been in charge of a foster/adopting in-taking home.

She has always reached out into helping the community, along with Pastor Dennis Spears Sr; who has been a mentor in the community for many years. Equally important, they both have been in charge and helped with food pantries, etc.

Jesus washed his disciple's feet to show the importance of serving. No man is greater than the other in the body of Christ. Our responsibilities may be greater, but we all were meant to serve.

Sound Doctrine Outreach Ministries has a great necessity to preach the true word, and also be as helpful as we can in our surrounding communities. We like to fellowship with others, and provide service through food drives, annual Men's fishing trips and much more.

Pastor Dennis Spears Sr., founded *"The Men's Adopt a Child For a Day Fishing Trip,"* many years ago. The importance of teaching a man how to fish, and he will be forever able to feed himself and live serves greatly. Even with deeper meaning, he encourages men to adopt a child for that day, but to also keep a relationship going with that individual for a lifetime. Each one teach one!

This Fishing Trip is every June, which falls on a Free Fishing Day; as well as a week or so near Father's Day. This is

just an example of the many

things that Sound Doctrine

Outreach Ministries provides for

its community in Milwaukee, WI.

Sound Doctrine has a mission

to complete for God.

Help be a part of our mission

today!

We have no extra agendas but to

serve!

GeT
INVOlVeD!

Membership

All are welcome to join our church family! We welcome you once, we welcome you twice, we welcome you three times in the name of Jesus Christ.

We have no respect of person, but we do want everyone to respect each other, and to understand that we are here to honor God's word, his rules, and to spread the honest Gospel.

Our leader Pastor Dennis Spears Sr., is not here to please the people but to lead the people according to the Sound Doctrine that Jesus demands for us to take heed to, as we live our Christian lives.

We are excited to have you as part of our church body. May God bless you!

Sound Doctrine
Outreach Ministries Inc.

For Questions/Concerns

Please Contact:

Darick Spears

Email: darick@ddsmediaworks.com

Website:

https://www.sounddocministry.com/

Facebook:

https://www.facebook.com/sounddoctrineoutreach/